Diving For All

by Alan Watkinson
with illustrations by Rico

Underwater World Publications Ltd

NOTE: Although reasonable care has been taken in preparing this book, the Publishers and Authors respectively accept no responsibility or liability for any errors, omissions, or alterations, or for any consequences ensuing upon the use of, or reliance upon, any information contained herein. Due caution should be exercised by anyone attempting dives. The reproduction by any means in whole or part of any content of the book is expressly forbidden without the written permission of Underwater World Publications Ltd.

Book designed and produced
by Liz Hopkinson

Cover photograph
by Mike Portelly

Illustrations
by Rico

Acknowledgements to the following for the use of photographs:
p.8   Dietmar Reimar
p.10 Dietmar Reimar
p.12 Imperial War Museum
p.13 Imperial War Museum
p.39 Fig 48 Typhoon International Ltd
p.40 Fig 50 Mike Todd
p.40 Fig 51 Typhoon International Ltd
p.45 Fig 58 Typhoon International Ltd

Typeset by New Rush Filmsetters Ltd
58-62 Folgate Street, London E1
and Printed by Butler and Tanner Ltd
Frome, Somerset

ISBN: 0 946020 10 8

CONTENTS

Part 3 PREPARING FOR THE ADVENTURE

Part 4 SENSE AND SAFETY

Part 5   THE GREAT ADVENTURE

ABOUT THE AUTHOR

Author Alan Watkinson is one of the most highly qualified sports divers — and diving instructors — in the world.

A member of the British Sub-Aqua Club for nearly 25 years, he was among the first of the few to have earned the 1st Class Diver qualification, and he is one of the still relatively rare people to hold the National Instructor rating, the BS-AC's highest instructor degree.

He is also a 4-Star World Underwater Federation Instructor, a Snorkel Instructor No.1, and a member of the International College of Instructors. He holds top Royal Lifesaving Society qualifications.

Alan has instructed and examined not only thoughout the UK, but also in the Cayman Islands, Cyprus, Germany, Hong Kong, Jamaica, Newfoundland, and elsewhere.

His wealth of experience and love of the sport have been combined in the writing of Diving For All.

FOREWORD

I find nowadays that I have fewer opportunities to go diving than I used to have when I was serving in the Royal Navy, but I enjoy it greatly when I have the chance.

It is such a different world underwater, a chance to come into contact with nature in a way that is denied to most, a chance to experience the amazing feeling of weightlessness that can only otherwise be achieved by astronauts.

I first began to dive when I was in the Royal Navy at the age of 21, following in the footsteps of my father and my great uncle, Lord Mountbatten, who were both enthusiasts.

Since then, I have dived in many different conditions, from well below freezing point underneath the Arctic ice in Canada, to the warm waters of the West Indies and the Pacific.

I found my dives on the wreck of the Mary Rose in the Solent particularly interesting, although the visibility underwater was appalling.

The underwater environment, the life it contains, the opportunities for exploration and discovery, and, especially, the challenge are all fascinating aspects of diving.

Today it is easier to enjoy this wonderful sport. The training is superb. The equipment is advanced. The opportunities to dive both at home and abroad are almost limitless.

I recommend this concise little book, which tells you with refreshing simplicity what you have to do to become a diver.

You never know, perhaps it will draw you into The Great Underwater Adventure!

Charles

His Royal Highness, The Prince of Wales

PART 1

INTRODUCTION

Diving is Fun

Diving like most adventure sports breeds comradeship: the very nature of the sport brings together kindred spirits. Families need not be exluded as most dive-sites, being situated by coast, lake or river, are pleasant places to be. Camping, beach-parties, club holidays and other compatible water sports are all part of the diving scene. Club nights, film shows, interesting talks and lectures can fill the winter evenings, maintaining interest throughout the year. Above all the sheer joy of being and seeing underwater is pleasure unsurpassed.

Diving is Interesting

Once the skills and drills have become second nature, as they soon will, the diver can turn his or her attention to one or more of the many interesting aspects of underwater exploration. Geology, marine biology, zoology, archaeology, photography: an impressive list of interests beckons.

Nor need the diver be an established expert. Skills may soon be acquired through courses in any of these underwater disciplines. Likewise the diver will become familiar with boat-handling, navigation, weather forecasting and even teaching as part of the ongoing involvement with the sport and the search for knowledge. The interest is there for those who pursue and persevere.

Diving is Adventure

In this shrinking world, fast jet planes carry passengers to the most remote corners of the earth in a matter of hours. Few secrets remain, few places are untrod by human foot, and only the highest mountains, the dense equatorial forests or remote deserts offer challenge to the land-bound exploring spirit. Yet for the trained sport diver adventure and exploration lie a few metres from any beach anywhere. For here starts the vast expanse that accounts for seven tenths of the surface of the earth.

Beyond the holiday-makers on the beach, a diver will find silence, peace, adventure and, during a brief sojourn, see some part of the earth's surface no other human has seen before. Not necessarily for a diver the costly expedition to faraway places: a few short hours after leaving desk or workbench he or she can be an explorer in the wonderful world that lies just below the surface of the sea.

Diving is for All

Diving is not the sport of the macho male braving the elements and fighting the denizens of the deep, and it never really has been. Forget the myths and Hollywood legends — diving is truly for everyone.

Providing a medical examination can be satisfied, *any* reasonably fit swimmer over 14 years of age can embark on a course of training and will soon be introduced to the fascinating world beneath the waves. For children younger than fourteen, this being the age when it is generally considered that disciplines and limitations will be understood and accepted, snorkel diving provides an interesting and enjoyable pastime that also allows the participant to view and enter this exciting new environment.

World War 2 frogman in the suit worn for attacking enemy ships.

History of Sport Diving

Diving has been practised in a variety of forms for centuries. Brave men using cumbersome and often extremely dangerous equipment have worked on shipwrecks, wrested treasure from the depths and performed extraordinary feats of civil engineering beneath the surface.

The unpleasant and risky nature of this work, coupled with restrictions of movement and vision imposed by the equipment, would have excluded any pleasure from the experience. The diver, tethered to the surface by his lifelines and air-supply hose, would have little time or enthusiasm for anything but the job in hand, his personal safety and his hopefully imminent return to the surface.

Nor was there much pleasure for the wartime "frogmen" or human torpedoes — known as "charioteers" — who, despite comparative freedom of movement afforded by portable oxygen sets and frogman's fins, were subject to depth limits because they were breathing undiluted oxygen. In addition, the discomfort of clammy so-called "dry" suits, to say nothing of the highly dangerous tasks they undertook, would distract the most romantic soul from the beauty which may have, at times, surrounded them.

Despite their wartime experiences — clamping magnetic mines to the undersides of enemy ships, cutting through anti-submarine

Royal Navy divers in World War 2 diving dress. A port clearance diver and, on the right, a human torpedo charioteer wearing a portable oxygen set.

13

Sport diver Jacques Cousteau and diver-journalist Peter Small.

nets or sitting astride as much as 500lb of high explosive contained within the human torpedo they steered — many of these ex-service divers, appreciating the potential of diving for sport, provided the hard core of early sport diving clubs which formed in the late 1940s.

The man who, without doubt, has been the most influential in the development of diving as a sport is Jacques Cousteau. His development of the aqualung as a portable underwater breathing system provided pure air on demand and at the correct pressure. This, with the addition of a face mask for clear vision and swim fins for ease of movement, provides the means for anyone with a spirit of adventure to explore the incredible world underwater.

In 1953 the father of British sport diving, Oscar Gugen, and diver-journalist Peter Small laid the foundations for what was to become the world's largest diving club. The British Sub-Aqua Club is recognised as the governing body for the sport in England and Wales, has branches in many parts of the world and, since its formation, has been dedicated to the development of training and safety standards which are second to none anywhere in the world.

Learning to Dive

Diving is not something that can or should be learned from a book. The only safe way to become a diver is under the guidance of an experienced diving instructor. This can be as a member of a recognised diving club or school.

Novice diver under instruction.

Don't be tempted to take short cuts. A friend who offers to take you diving may not be as experienced as his expensive equipment suggests. Having started on a course in a class, stay with it. The trainee who drops out, thinking he knows enough, may discover to his cost that the solution to his first diving problem was covered in the lesson he missed. There are "risks" in diving, as in any adventure sport, but by far the greatest danger is ignorance. The well-trained diver who follows the basic diving safety rules can relax and enjoy the sport while always diving within his limitations.

Time spent learning to dive, be it in school or club, is always time well spent. It will also be fun. From the first thrill of seeing a rusty but clearly focused hairpin on the pool bottom, to the indescribable pleasure of the first dive in the open sea with living fish — every moment will be sheer pleasure for the true enthusiast. Don't rush; enjoy and learn from each lesson and benefit from the experience.

PART 2

FIRST THINGS FIRST

Choosing and Using Basic Equipment

Ease of movement and clear vision are basic essentials of any diving experience. It follows therefore that a mastery of the equipment that provides these is the first requirement for a trainee diver.

FINS

Moving around in the water is made very easy by adding a paddle to the foot. This paddle or "fin" provides the diver with such an advantage that he no longer needs, nor should he use, his arms for swimming.

The noun "fin" is preferred to "flipper" if for no better reason than that the verb is more pronounceable. A fin is an extension of the diver's foot, providing more surface area.

Fins come in a variety of shapes, sizes and fittings. Selection will be mainly one of personal choice, but consider the following points:

FIT: When choosing a pair of fins the future use of diving socks or bootees should be allowed for. The adjustable fin will fit over a variation of footwear. Fins must be comfortable and never overtight. A tight fin will start by being uncomfortable and progress

to becoming excruciating — causing foot cramp and a ruined dive.
SIZE AND STYLE: The larger the area provided by the fins the
more power and speed can be generated, *but* the more effort will
be required to propel them. Therefore a compromise is recommended, large enough for best advantage without strain.
THE SHOE-FITTING FIN provides a pocket into which the foot
fits like wearing a shoe, the open toe style is obviously more comfortable. This type of fin needs to be a good fit as no adjustment
is possible.

Fig 1

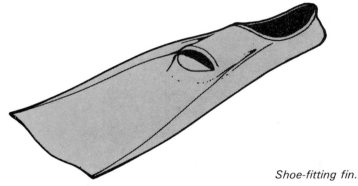

Shoe-fitting fin.

FINS WITH ADJUSTABLE HEELSTRAPS provide a pocket for
the front half of the foot, with a strap that fits around the heel holding the fin in place.

Fig 2

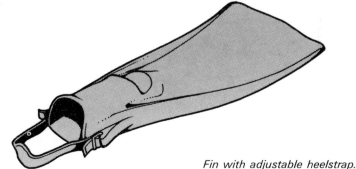

Fin with adjustable heelstrap.

18

JET FINS, which have louvres in the blades and allow water to pass through on the upstroke, reduce the effort required to propel an otherwise rather large fin.

Fig 3

Jet fin.

LONG RACING STYLE FINS have no place in a normal diver's kitbag; these are specialised items of equipment designed for surface fin racing.

Fig 4

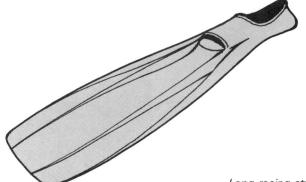

Long racing style fin.

MASKS

Without the ability to see underwater, sport diving becomes a pointless exercise: the human eye will not focus in water. A diving facemask, which encloses eyes and nose, provides a pocket of air in which the eye can function normally. Air blown out through the nose provides a simple pressure-compensating system, enabling the diver to equalise pressure inside the mask with that of the surrounding water.

TYPES OF MASK:

For safety's sake, choose a mask that has a toughened glass faceplate. An adjustable retaining strap is essential, preferably one that is split or double at the back of the head. Your mask should also have access for nose pinching: usually two small pockets, one each side of the nose, that allow you to pinch your nose from outside the mask. This will help you clear your ears when pressure starts to increase (a technique that will be explained later in this book).

Figs 5 & 6

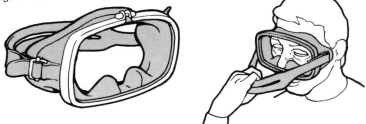

Choose a mask with a toughened glass faceplace and adjustable strap.

Though masks may vary in appearance they differ little in function. A good mask should fit well onto the face. To check this, place mask in position making sure no wisps of hair are trapped between face and mask. Without fitting the retaining strap, breathe in through the nose. The mask should stay in place until you breathe out again.

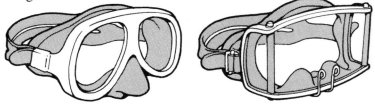

Figs 7 & 8   *Your mask should have access for nose pinching.*

20

SNORKEL TUBES

A snorkel tube is a simple device designed to facilitate safe and comfortable breathing when swimming in choppy water or in a face-down position. The snorkel tube's secret is its simplicity: little more than an open-ended tube with a soft rubber mouthpiece and a "U" or "V" bend to trap droplets of water which may have entered through the open end or remained after tube clearing.

Extras such as clearing valves or anti-flooding devices are no substitute for good clearing techniques. They can be dangerous and should be avoided.

Fig 9

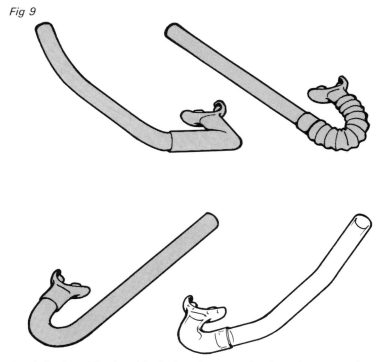

Snorkel tubes. The bend is designed to trap droplets of water and prevent the snorkeller from breathing them in.

Getting to Know your Basic Equipment

One of the most important stages in learning to dive is the mastery of basic equipment: mask, fins and snorkel tube. These three items will be used every time a diver enters the water. Good finning, mask and tube clearing techniques are essential for the diver's future comfort and safety.

Different instructors may teach the use of each item in varying order; the following is just one sequence.

FINNING

Fins are designed for swimming, not walking, and should be fitted as near to the edge of the water as is practical. Wet both foot and fin before fitting.

Fig 10

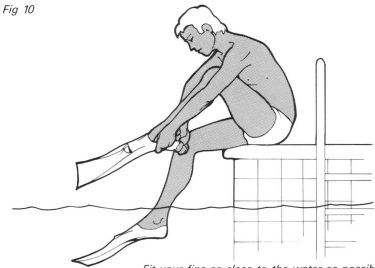

Fit your fins as close to the water as possible.

Once in the water practise finning in the following way: keep legs straight, use all the leg from the hip down and allow only slight knee bending. Don't cycle with legs and — above all — keep the fins in and under the water. When finning, arms should be kept by the side or held behind the back. Holding the head and shoulders high will help keep fins underwater.

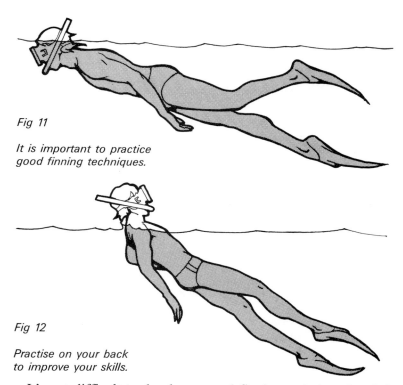

Fig 11

It is important to practice good finning techniques.

Fig 12

Practise on your back to improve your skills.

It's not difficult to develop a good finning technique but it is very worthwhile. To further develop finning skills, practise finning on the back. A little more knee bending will be required in this position.

If walking in fins, either in or out of the water, is unavoidable, walk backwards keeping a lookout for obstructions. There is much less chance of an undignified or painful tumble.

FITTING THE MASK AND SNORKEL
Standing in shallow water, prepare the mask by spreading a thin layer of saliva inside the mask faceplate and rinse the mask with water. This will reduce misting problems. Now place the mask in position, making sure that no hair is trapped between the mask and face as this will allow water to leak into the mask. Finally, put the strap around the back of the head fairly high up. The strap should be adjusted so as to hold the mask firmly but not tightly in place.

An over-tight mask will distort and leak as well as being uncomfortable. Putting your face down into the water will prove the seal of the mask. Should there be any leaks, first check for stray hair, then adjust until watertight.

Figs 13, 14 & 15

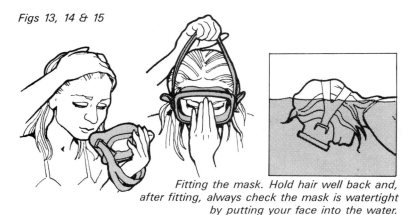

Fitting the mask. Hold hair well back and, after fitting, always check the mask is watertight by putting your face into the water.

Next fit the snorkel tube by slipping the tube under the mask strap at the side of the head. Now place the mouthpiece in position with its sealing flange behind the lips, holding the rubber pips gently with the teeth.

The comfort of the fit will confirm whether the snorkel should be on the left or right side of the head.. With your head still out of the water, practise breathing or, more accurately, sucking air through the tube. Progress by submerging face mask. You should carry on breathing through the tube without water entering.

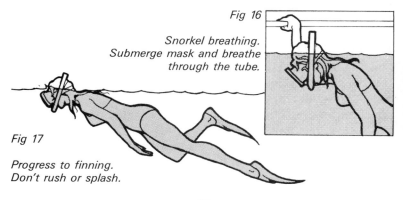

Fig 16

Snorkel breathing. Submerge mask and breathe through the tube.

Fig 17

Progress to finning. Don't rush or splash.

Now for more finning practice, this time with mask and snorkel in place. Concentrate on a steady breathing rhythm with controlled finning action. Don't rush or splash. You are now well on the way to becoming a competent snorkeller.

FLOODED MASK OR SNORKEL

Should water enter the mask simply turn over on your back, lift the bottom edge of mask and let the water drain out. Water in the snorkel tube will be expelled quickly by a good hard blow.

SNORKEL CLEARING

In order to enjoy snorkel sport to the full you will wish to descend below the surface. To do this two new techniques need to be acquired: snorkel clearing and surface dives.

The open-ended snorkel tube will fill with water once below the surface. This water must obviously be cleared before breathing can continue once the surface has been regained. This is done by blowing the water from the tube using a sharp, blasting exhalation. One good blow is usually adequate. However, the first breath you take should be tentative so as not to inhale any water left behind. If needed, a second blow will clear the residue.

Fig 18   *Fig 19*

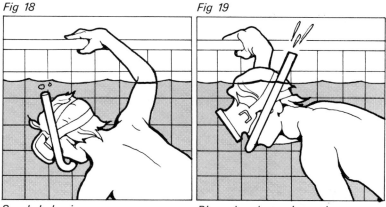

Snorkel clearing.
Below the surface the tube
will fill with water.

Blow sharply to clear tube.
Practice these techniques first in
shallow water.

Practise this technique in shallow water, for example holding onto the side of a swimming pool: duck under water allowing water to flood the tube, then surface and clear. Now swim around on the surface, remove snorkel from the mouth, flood, replace and clear. Clearing will soon become second nature, then you may venture below the surface.

PART 3

PREPARING FOR THE ADVENTURE

Diving

SURFACE DIVE

The technique of diving below the surface is described variously as a Duck Dive, Jacknife or Surface Dive. This requires practice in order that the dive can be accomplished in one neat movement, ensuring that the diver won't become exhausted by unnecessary exertion, nor will the fish be put to flight by a clumsy intrusion.

Fig 20

Surface Dive, Duck Dive or Jacknife.
Lie on the surface, bend waist and point
arms down. Lift legs and fins into the air.

Start your dive by lying prone on the surface. Now bend at the waist, arms pointing straight down, simultaneously lift legs and fins straight up into the air. In this vertical position the weight of legs and fins will push you down.

Once the fins have become submerged, start finning downwards; level out and fin a short distance then head back to the surface. The snorkel tube can now be "cleared" as previously practised.

Persevere with your surface dive until it can regularly be accomplished with the minimum disturbance of water.

FEET-FIRST DIVE

This dive is carried out in the following way: start in an upright position, fin hard so that as much of you as possible comes out of the water. Now stop finning, breathe out and allow yourself to sink. Once totally submerged, bend at the waist and fin downwards.

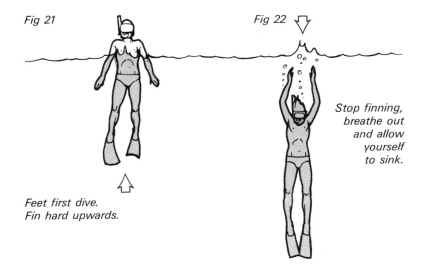

Fig 21

Fig 22

Stop finning, breathe out and allow yourself to sink.

Feet first dive.
Fin hard upwards.

Advanced Snorkelling Techniques

Having become proficient in the basics of snorkel diving it is well worth acquiring a number of more advanced techniques. The following drills are not difficult but will prepare the snorkeller for most eventualities and for advancement to aqualung diving.

MOUTH BREATHING

A snorkeller or aqualung diver is obviously breathing through the mouth only, the diving mask conveniently preventing water from entering the nose. If, however, the mask becomes flooded or dislodged it is important that mouth-only breathing continues. The following drill will ensure competence in this technique.

Standing in shallow water, remove mask holding snorkel tube in place and submerge face so that mouth and unprotected nose are below the surface. Practise breathing so that no water enters nose. If you suck air through the tube, as if drinking through a straw, the nose will tend to close automatically and no water will enter. Practise this drill until you are able to fin around on the surface without your mask, breathing comfortably through your mouth.

DISPLACEMENT SNORKEL CLEARING

When surfacing from a snorkel dive, tilt head well back so that you are looking towards the surface. Just before reaching the surface, breathe out gently through the snorkel. As soon as you break surface, flip the head forward still exhaling. Now take first breath without the need for the usual hard blow.

Fig 23

Displacement snorkel clearing. Tilt head well back, and still below surface, breathe out gently.

MOBILITY

The ability to perform smooth forward and backward rolls underwater is a good confidence builder, developing control, balance and orientation.

FORWARD ROLLS: These are best performed as an extension of a surface dive. Once completely below the surface, tuck head down and chin into the chest. Without the use of fins, use your extended arms to pull you round in a neat forward roll.

Fig 24

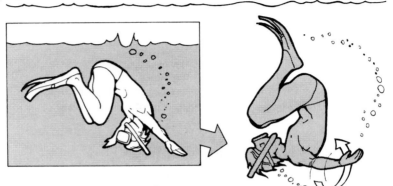

Forward rolls below the surface.

BACKWARD ROLLS: As with forward rolls, start with a surface dive. This time, with head held well back, arch your back, again stretch arms out but revolve in the opposite direction.

Fig 25

Backward rolls.

ENTERING AND LEAVING THE WATER: Whenever possible walk into the water. Your fins should be fitted just before entering or even while standing in shallow water. Should you need to jump into the water make absolutely sure that there are no obstructions, human or otherwise, below. Holding mask and snorkel in place, step well out remembering to hold your breath. Enter the water with fins pointing downwards to assist in a clean entry.

Fig 26

Jump entry holding mask and snorkel in place.

If walking when leaving the water, remove your fins as soon as it is safe to do so. If you are walking with fins on, remember to walk backwards. When leaving deep water your fins will help you to fin up and out of the water. Once safely sitting on poolside, boat or rocks remove fins.

Fig 27

When walking with fins on, walk backwards.

Your mask and snorkel tube should remain in position until you are safely out of the water.

SNORKELLING IN OPEN WATER

Once pool or sheltered water training is complete, you are ready to progress to open water. It may be the sea, a lake or a river. Whichever, you will now need to invest in some extra equipment. In all but the warmest climates you will need a diving suit. Because a suit will make you buoyant you will also need a weight belt and you will certainly need a lifejacket or buoyancy compensator.

DIVING SUITS: A suit can be "dry", which means that water can't normally enter due to seals at neck wrists and ankles, or "wet". A wetsuit is made of neoprene which allows water to enter but, due to the close fit, only as a thin film. This film of water rapidly warms to body temperature and keeps the diver warm for reasonable periods, dependent on the season and the temperature of the surrounding water. Hoods, bootees and gloves will be required with both types of suit.

Fig 28

Wetsuit.

Fig 29

Dry suit.

32

WEIGHT BELTS: A belt supporting a selection of lead weights will be required in order to compensate for the buoyancy of the diving suit. Two very important points must be remembered about weight belts:

1 *The belt must always be fitted with a quick release mechanism.*
2 *The belt must always be unobstructed by other equipment so that it can be removed instantly.*

Fig 30

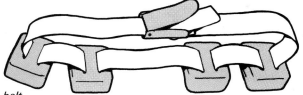

Weight belt.

LIFEJACKETS: A lifejacket or buoyancy compensator should always be worn in open water. It will need an inflation system which can easily be operated by the diver or a companion. The jacket should support the diver in a head up, face out of the water position.

Fig 31   Fig 32

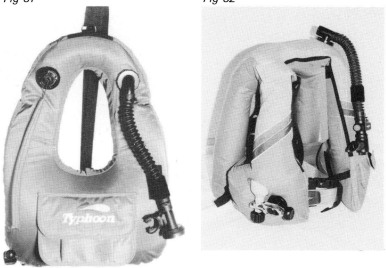

Adjustable buoyancy life jacket — ABLJ (Adjustable buoyancy life jacket) and Stab (stablising) jacket with cylinder. Both can be inflated underwater.

These three items of extra equipment should be tried out in safe water before venturing further.

Signals

Once in the water, mask and mouthpiece in place, it is most difficult, if not impossible, to communicate vocally; even on the surface it is not recommended that divers remove their mouthpiece. Therefore a system of hand signals has been devised and should be understood by all divers, including snorkel divers.

Most hand signals are self-explanatory and will be understood by divers throughout the world. Spend a little time memorising and practising these and you will become multilingual in or under the water.

DIVER TO DIVER SIGNALS

Signals must be transmitted accurately and clearly. They should be given face to face, from diver to diver, and repeated by the recipient to ensure they have been understood. It will be seen that signals fall into two basic categories: NORMAL and EMERGENCY.

NORMAL SIGNALS cover instructions and questions such as: "Are you OK?", which when repeated indicates "Yes, I am OK", and "Go up", "Go down", "Go that way", etc.

EMERGENCY SIGNALS indicate such emergency situations as "Something is wrong", "I am in distress", "I am out of air", etc.

THE BUDDY SYSTEM: Now is a good time to remember the diver's Golden Rule: *"Never Dive Alone."* Even when snorkelling, pair up with a buddy. Each buddy will look to the safety of the other. There should also be a cover on the shore who will keep an eye on the snorkellers and ensure their safe return.

It is important that a buddy takes immediate action when given an emergency signal.

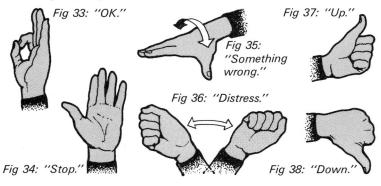

Fig 33: "OK."

Fig 35: "Something wrong."

Fig 37: "Up."

Fig 36: "Distress."

Fig 34: "Stop."

Fig 38: "Down."

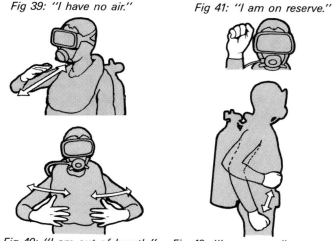

Fig 39: "I have no air." Fig 41: "I am on reserve."

Fig 40: "I am out of breath." Fig 42: "I cannot pull my reserve."

The above are the basic hand signals which must be learned, understood and remembered. Other local or special signals can be devised, providing all divers know and understand their meaning.

DIVER TO SURFACE COVER SIGNALS

Divers and snorkellers will need to communicate with companions on the shore or in boats, who are known as the surface cover party. The signals used will, in most cases, be restricted to those indicating the diver's well-being. These are given with arms held high and clear of the water. A diver who surfaces and neither gives nor responds to signals must be assumed to be in need of assistance.

Diver's signals to surface cover party:

Fig 43: "I am OK." Fig 44: "I am in distress."

LIGHT SIGNALS

At night, signals may be given by torch light using the diving torch which must be carried by every diver when night-diving. Usual signals are used, illuminated by pointing the torch at the signalling hand. Care must be taken not to allow the torch to shine into the eyes of your companion and dazzle him.

Diver to cover party signals are given using the torch directed towards shore or boat.

Light signals:

Fig 45: "I am OK."   Fig 46: "I am in distress."

SOUND SIGNALS

Sound signals, other than hi-tech in-water communication systems, such as tapping a cylinder with a diving knife or banging two rocks together, are primitive and really can only be used to attract attention. Some boats may carry fireworks which will explode below the surface to recall divers; pre-determined revving of the boat engine may be used for the same purpose.

More advanced signals may be given by rope. These will be discussed later.

Coping with Pressure

Before venturing below the surface, it is important that the effects of pressure upon the body and equipment of the diver and snorkeller are understood.

Pressure is basically the result of the weight of surrounding water. As a diver descends, so the weight of water above, and therefore the pressure, will increase.

It is an interesting and relevant fact that the weight and pressure of the atmosphere that surrounds the earth is doubled by a descent to only 10 metres (33 feet) below the surface. The pressure on the surface is known as barometric pressure or 1 bar. At 10 metres below the surface it will be 2 bar, and is known as "total" or "absolute" pressure which is the sum of the water pressure plus that of the atmosphere above it. For every 10 metres of depth increase, one more bar will be added.

It will be easily understood that any compressible object or substance below the surface will be squeezed and reduced in size: the deeper — the more pressure — the smaller it becomes. Air, being compressible, will be affected in this way. See Fig 47. This in turn creates a number of problems for the diver to resolve. Probably the first effects of pressure experienced will be "mask squeeze" and pressure on the ears and sinus.

Fig 47

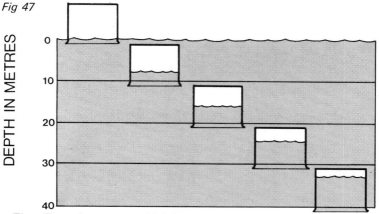

The effect of pressure, which increases with depth, is compression.

MASK SQUEEZE

A diving mask — having flexible sides and normally containing air — will start to collapse on to the face once under water. If no corrective action is taken the sides will distort and water may enter or eyes may be damaged by the increased pressure. However, it is a simple matter to equalise the pressure inside the mask by gently exhaling through the nose. This action should be taken before the effects of pressure are felt, then repeated during the descent.

EARS AND SINUS SQUEEZE

Air spaces contained within the skull are the inner ear and the sinus

37

passages. The air within these spaces will compress painfully if not relieved. Fortunately, these are connected by passages called Eustachian Tubes to the back of the throat. Air which has been compressed within the lungs, is able to enter the air spaces via these tubes equalising the pressure. This equalisation can often be accomplished by simply swallowing hard causing the Eustachian Tubes to open. Should this not be sufficient, pinch the nose using the thumb sockets, thoughtfully provided by the mask manufacturer, and blow gently down the nose. This creates a back pressure that causes the ears to "pop", indicating that the pressure on each side of the eardrum has equalised. If this does not work don't persist — you may cause damage.

A diver with a cold will suffer swelling within the area of the nose and Eustachian Tubes. This swelling will affect the ability to "clear ears". There is also the danger of pushing infection through into the inner ear. Therefore, no attempt should be made to dive when suffering from a cold.

SUIT COMPRESSION
A diving suit will be affected by pressure as the gas in the bubbles, which are part of wetsuit construction, or the air that is inevitably trapped inside a drysuit, will compress and therefore reduce the inherent buoyancy of the suit. The deeper the diver, the greater the pressure, the less buoyancy provided by the suit. This loss of buoyancy can obviously be dangerous and is one of a number of very good reasons for the wearing of buoyancy compensators or lifejackets and for exercising great care when adjusting weight.

Aqualung Diving

Having mastered the techniques of basic equipment, the snorkel diver will soon be spending longer spells exploring the underwater world and will obviously feel the need to spend more time in this fascinating new environment. The limitations of breath-hold diving, requiring the snorkeller to return frequently to the surface to rest and refill lungs with air, can obviously be overcome by carrying a portable air supply.

THE AQUALUNG

The equipment required to take air below the surface is the aqualung or, as it is known in the United States, Scuba (self-contained underwater breathing apparatus). This equipment comprises three main components:

THE CYLINDER is made from steel or aluminium alloy. This cylinder, which is manufactured specifically for diving use and to very high specifications, will carry a series of letters and numbers, usually stamped on the shoulder. These provide important information regarding date of manufacture, capacity, working and test pressure. This information should be known and understood.

The cylinder will be capable of holding air at very high pressure, probably 200 times that of atmospheric air, possibly even more. Remembering that the pressure of atmospheric air is one bar, it will be readily understood that the pressure inside such a cylinder will be 200 bar. This amount of air would last a diver approximately 200 times longer than the same volume of non-compressed air, providing it was breathed at sea level.

It is important to remember that this air endurance will be reduced as a diver descends. For example, the absolute pressure on the diver at 10 metres will be 2 bars, so it will take twice the air from the cylinder to fill the lungs at this depth. At 30 metres the surrounding pressure becomes 4 bar, four times that at the surface. The diver's air will now only last one-quarter of the time it would have at sea

Fig 48

DIVE DURATION TABLE

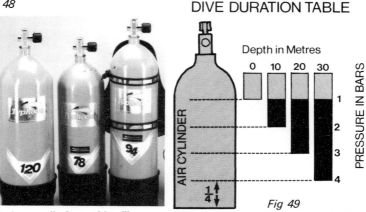

Aqualung cylinders with pillar valves.

The endurance of compressed air is reduced as the diver descends.

level. From this it will be seen that depth of dive and air endurance are inexorably linked and must be carefully calculated before each dive.

Each cylinder is fitted with a valve designed to hold back the high-pressure air until required.

THE DEMAND VALVE or diving regulator, as it is also known, is the second essential component of the aqualung. This valve is capable of providing the diver with air from the cylinder at the required pressure on demand as it is sensitive to both the surrounding pressure and to the diver's breathing requirements. The invention of the demand valve provided the breakthrough which made free diving, without the encumbrance of surface air lines, possible.

The compressed air contained within the cylinder is reduced in pressure, usually in two stages. The first stage, attached to the cylinder valve, reduces the high-pressure air down to a medium pressure. The air then passes through a medium-pressure hose to the second stage which is fitted with a mouthpiece. Here the pressure is again reduced, this time to that of the surrounding water and the air can be breathed comfortably by the diver.

The mouth-held second stage is fitted with an exhaust valve enabling the disposal of the diver's expired air. A purge button is fitted to the front or side of the second stage and allows water to be purged from a flooded second stage. This technique will be discussed in AQUALUNG DIVING TECHNIQUES.

Fig 50   *Fig 51*

Single hose demand valve.
Photo: Mike Todd.

Twin cylinder set with demand valve.

40

THE HARNESS means the aqualung may be transported easily above and below the water. This consists of a band or bands to secure the cylinder and a selection of shoulder, waist and jock straps to fit the unit to the diver's back. The main considerations are that the harness should be comfortable and easy to fit and remove both in and out of the water. The fastening for the harness must be designed for quick release.

RESERVE VALVES AND CONTENTS GAUGES

The ability to know how much air is in the cylinder at any time is essential. An accurate pressure gauge connected to the aqualung will indicate at a glance the pressure of the air within the cylinder. See Fig 58. This information enables the diver to determine when he must commence his return to the surface. A reserve valve system, frequently used by continental divers, is fitted with a restrictor. When breathing becomes difficult the diver can open the restrictor by pulling the reserve lever. There will now be sufficient air for a normal ascent to the surface. The efficiency of the reserve system depends on the diver ensuring that the lever is set before the dive commences. Failing to do this could result in no warning of falling pressure and no reserve air.

Aqualung Diving Techniques

The skilled snorkeller is more than halfway to becoming an aqualung diver. Finning, surface diving and mobility technique are basically the same with or without an aqualung. Additional skills such as clearing unwanted water from mask and regulator and the important technique of buddy breathing, which is sharing one aqualung between two divers, can soon be accomplished.

FAMILIARISATION AND BUOYANCY CONTROL

Once the assembly of the aqualung has been sorted out, by checking there are no leaks, straps are adjusted and the set fitting comfortably, the next stage is to familiarise yourself with breathing from the regulator. Do this first on dry land, then kneeling in shallow water with your head just below the surface. Concentrate on breathing out. This requires a little more effort than normal but

Fig 52

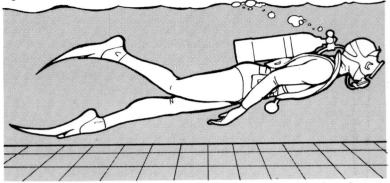

Practise in very shallow water until breathing from the aqualung is natural. Adjust weights until you have good buoyancy control.

the inhalations will take care of themselves. Still in very shallow water practise finning along on the bottom until breathing from the aqualung is as normal as breathing fresh air on the surface.

Before venturing further, it is time to sort out buoyancy: adding or removing weights until you are able to control your buoyancy simply by breathing in and out. Lying on the bottom, by taking a deep breath from the aqualung, you should lift off. Breathe out and you should sink back down again. This buoyancy control is very important and time should be spent getting it right.

MASK AND MOUTHPIECE CLEARING

Still in very shallow water, mask and mouthpiece clearing techniques should now be learned.

MASK CLEARING: This is simply the process of replacing any water, that may have entered the mask, with air from the diver's lungs, by exhaling through the nose. This is best accomplished by holding the head back so that the face plate is as near parallel to the surface of the water as possible. Press the top edge of the mask gently against the forehead and exhale through the nose. This air will displace any water that is in the mask. See Fig 53.

Practise by allowing more water to enter and clearing until you are able to flood the mask completely and empty it with one breath. The next stage of progression is to remove the mask, replace and clear. When replacing the mask care should be taken that hair is not trapped between mask-seal and face, this will create leaks. Re-fit in the following sequence: See Figs 54−57 opposite.

Fig 53

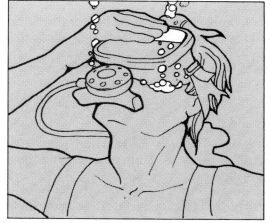

Mask clearing underwater. Press top of mask and exhale through the nose.

Figs 54–57

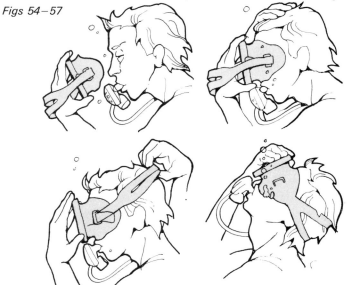

Refitting and clearing mask under water.

1 *Hold mask with its strap around the back of your hand.*
2 *Push hair up off forehead and hold it out of the way.*
3 *Place mask in position on face.*
4 *Lift strap over onto back of head.*
5 *Clear water as previously practised.*

MOUTHPIECE CLEARING: The small amount of water which may enter the regulator mouthpiece will normally empty if you blow hard. To prepare for buddy-breathing practise by removing the mouthpiece, then press the purge button so that it bubbles. Replace the mouthpiece at the same time removing your finger from the purge. The mouthpiece should be water free.

IMPORTANT — COMPRESSED AIR

In previous chapters we have discussed the relevance of pressure to the diver and his equipment. It is imperative that the diver breathing compressed air understands that just as air is compressed within the diver's body when he descends, so it will expand when he ascends. Therefore, air taken from an aqualung below the surface to fill the lungs will, if not exhaled, expand beyond the capacity of the lungs with tragic and often fatal results. No diver must go below the surface without understanding this fact and knowing that under no circumstances should the breath be held when ascending.

Once the foregoing is understood the diver may venture into deeper water to practice finning, clearing, surface diving and mobility.

Other Equipment

Most diving equipment is obviously essential: without a mask — what's the point? Without fins you'll be too slow; without a suit too cold and without an aqualung you could only make a very short dive!

There are, however, a selection of equipment items not so obvious but equally essential. The lifejacket we have discussed, but who can guess depth and time accurately? A diving watch and a depth guage, or equivalent equipment, are essential in order that decompression problems (the Bends) can be avoided.

DIVING WATCH

The main requirement of any watch for diving is that it must be both waterproof and capable of withstanding pressure. Many so-called waterproof watches look the part but are not suitable for the purpose.

Buy yours from a dive shop or a jeweller who genuinely understands and will guarantee his product. Digital or traditional? It doesn't matter as long as the watch can be easily read, sometimes in low visibility or even darkness. The strap should be adjustable; remember you will want it to fit your wrist with or without a suit.

DEPTH GAUGE

Basically, you usually get what you pay for. Again consider readability. It is better to have clear numbers down to 40 metres than small numbers down to 80 metres that are hard to read and that you won't need anyway.

Depth gauges are finely tuned instruments that need treating with care. A small transportation box lined with sorbo rubber or similar is well worth acquiring or making. The gauge should also be checked for accuracy and calibrated at least once a season. Your dealer will advise you.

Fig 58

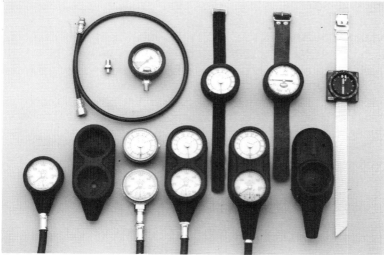

Selection of depth and pressure gauges.

COMPASS

A diving compass is mainly used for out and home navigation, but experienced divers can often get lost in much more complicated ways. A compass is not a magic charm that, if worn, will bring the diver back to the point of entry. Practise and it will be worth its weight in load stone.

45

KNEE PADS
Neopreen sleeves pulled over knees to protect expensive suit and delicate divers' knees from wear and tear.

GOODIE BAGS
A net bag is useful for keeping goodies in. It will also tend to get snagged on boats, wrecks and buddies' diving equipment!

CRAB HOOK
For persuading crabs to leave home or encouraging lobsters out of holes.

FLUORESCENT HOODS
Well worth wearing, this type of hood or hood cover enables the diver to be seen over long distances. An obvious safety device, an added advantage is that it distinguishes divers from seals during the rutting season!

SURFACE MARKER BUOY
Ideally, this location and monitoring system consists of a high visability buoy, a line and a reel. The advantage of using an S.M.B. is that the surface party is constantly aware of the diver's position and can, if necessary, send signals down the line. Highly recommended for almost all diving situations, and is essential for drift diving. See Fig 59.

Despite the apparent simplicity of this device, it is strongly recommended that training and practice should take place. The importance of good reeling, unreeling and handling techniques can't be overemphasised. There is a risk of entanglement in one's own safety line, but this will be avoided if the following basic instructions are followed:

1 *The buddy should swim, descend and ascend on the opposite side to that where the reel or winding device is carried.*
2 *Feet-first descent will reduce chance of line snagging on pillar valve or regulator.*
3 *Keep line fairly taut during ascent and descent.*
4 *When on bottom allow some, but not too much, spare line to cater for small variations in depth.*

Fig 59

Surface marker buoy system.

FIX PALMS
A sort of "Y" shaped rubber band designed to help retain slipper-type fins and for trapping fingers.

DIVING KNIFE
A diving knife should always be carried and always where it can easily be reached. Leg or arm sheaths are the most popular mounting. A knife which is carried on the leg will be less likely to snag if worn on the inside of the leg. A knife to be worn on the arm will be a short bladed variety and would normally be worn on the inside of the left forearm (opposite for left handers).

A sharp blade is essential as is a serrated cutting edge, as the most likely use for the diver's knife is cutting free of entanglements — not, as often supposed by onlookers, for killing sharks!

Fig 60

Diving knives.

PART 4

SENSE AND SAFETY

Avoiding Incidents

Prevention is always preferable to cure! Many potential diving incidents could, and should, be avoided by careful preparation, attention to detail, and observation of the rules of diving safety.
 Start your preparation for a dive in the following manner:
1 *Are you fit to dive? Not tired, overstressed, overfed, under the influence of drugs or alcohol or unwell? Even a common cold should exclude you.*
2 *Are conditions right for diving? Check sea condition, tidal state, weather conditions. Will they remain so for at least the duration of your dive?*
3 *Does your training and experience qualify you to take part in the dive? Take depth, general conditions, dive site and possible visibility into account.*
4 *Is your equipment fit for the dive? Do you have enough air? Does your suit provide enough insulation? Will a buddy-line be required to maintain contact?*
5 *Have you checked your equipment; It **must** all work well. No bodging up just for this dive! Is every part of your equipment correctly adjusted? A fin or mask strap that's just hanging on will almost certainly come adrift once you enter the water.*
Only if you can say "Yes" to all these questions should you proceed.

THE BUDDY CHECK

The next stage in preparing for a safe dive is a short but thorough pre-dive buddy check. This will ensure that both you and your buddy are ready to proceed. It won't take long but is another vital step in accident and incident prevention.

SAFETY: Confirm that both parties are aware of all safety drills and any possible hazards that could be encountered.

EXERCISE OR EXPEDITION: Where are you going? How long for? What are you going to do?

EQUIPMENT: You know your equipment is O.K. Show your buddy and let him or her show you.

DISCIPLINE: A question of deciding who will lead and who will follow. Two leaders just won't work.

SIGNALS: A reminder and time to confirm any extra or special signals that may be used.

Once ready to dive there is one more essential ingredient for safe diving — Don't Rush! Rushing will, at best, take the fun out of what should be a relaxing and pleasurable event and, at worst, lead you into an incident or accident.

Self Help

The single most important safety element in diving is probably the Buddy System, whereby ever diver has another acting as a guardian. This system will obviously only be effective if both parties recognise and accept their responsibility to each other.

This includes checking a buddy's status by giving and responding to regular O.K. signals, ensuring that a buddy does not inadvertently swim into danger, and maintaining visual or physical contact. Always maintain an awareness of one another's safety and be immediately willing to provide any assistance required.

Even a trainee diver has a responsibility for the instructor once out in open water and should have some knowledge and basic technical ability to understand and react to an emergency situation.

Basic life-saving techniques should be part of any training programme. At the very least these should include lifting, supporting, towing and helping to remove a subject from danger, and preferably will include other live-saving skills such as Expired Air Resuscitation and External Cardiac Massage.

Recognising and Reacting to Emergency Situations

Emergencies frequently grow out of very minor incidents. A dislodged or flooded mask, unexpected water entering the mouthpiece, over-exertion or a minor entanglement in seaweed are all situations that the diver-training programme should have prepared the diver to deal with.

However, a combination of these events can escalate leading to more serious problems and, eventually, to the diver's greatest enemy: 'PANIC'. Therefore, the first action in any incident is to stop, think, and remember the training drill. In most cases the diver has the training to resolve the problem, providing panic isn't allowed to set in.

A trained diver has probably removed and refitted a mask numerous times during training, so why should clearing a flooded mask in slightly deeper water prove any more difficult? Frantically tugging a slight entanglement will only make it worse. Calm reactions, careful appraisal and gentle actions will almost certainly resolve the problem, and there is always a buddy close at hand to offer assistance should that become necessary.

If the emergency requires an immediate return to the surface a normal ascent must, where practicable, be the first choice. If this isn't possible the most suitable type of emergency ascent should be carried out. An uncontrolled rush to the surface must be avoided at all costs. A correctly performed emergency ascent will, in all but the most extreme circumstances, ensure a safe return to the surface.

And Helping Others

An observant buddy will soon spot the early signs of difficulty in a companion: hasty and erratic actions, failure to respond to signals, and, of course, a direct signalled request for help. Once you are aware that your buddy requires your assistance make it immediately obvious that you understand the need and are taking action.

Your calm and logical actions are most important and should

be obvious. Assess what needs to be done, assisting in a way that will neither lead you into unreasonable danger nor cause your companion to panic.

HELPING AT THE SURFACE

Should a diver require help on the surface the two most important actions on behalf of a rescuer are:

1 *To make sure the distressed diver remains on the surface by providing buoyancy. This can mean inflating the subject's life jacket, or dry suit, removing the weight belt, or simply supporting the distressed diver yourself.*

2 *Summoning help. If there is a diving-boat giving cover or other boats around, signal the emergency. Other divers, snorkellers or swimmers can also be asked for assistance as can the shore party, if in sight.*

If help is not immediately available it may be necessary to tow the subject to safety. Correct towing methods are part of all good diver lifesaving training. But the basic requirement is to move in such a way that the face, particularly the mouth and nose, are clear of the water and that both rescuer and rescued have sufficient buoyancy.

More advanced training will include methods of giving expired air resuscitation whilst in the water, and lessons in landing and after care. It is the responsibility of every diver to become as proficient in lifesaving as possible, and — like First Aid — it's a good and useful social asset.

Fig 61   *Fig 62*

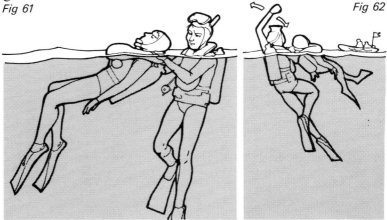

Make sure the distressed diver stays on the surface.   *Rescuing buddy summons help.*

Emergency Ascents

In the unlikely event that an equipment malfunction deprives a diver of his or her air supply, or that a diver, through careless planning or lack of attention to the contents guage, runs out of air, there are a number of actions which can be taken.

FREE ASCENT

This type of ascent involves swimming back to the surface in a controlled ascent, ensuring that the expanding air in the lungs is allowed to escape, by gently breathing out all the way up. Self-control and a complete lack of panic are required for this type of emergency ascent.

BUOYANT ASCENT

This uses the buoyancy of an adjustable buoyancy life jacket, buoyancy compensator, by drysuit inflation or dumping the weightbelt. The ascent must be controlled, and practice in the use of buoyancy systems is essential. A diver who wishes to drop the weightbelt to gain buoyancy in an emergency should, after releasing the belt's quick-release fastening, hold the belt at arm's length before letting it go. This will ensure that the belt does not snag on other equipment.

ASSISTED ASCENT

This type of emergency ascent can only be carried out with the assistance of a buddy, and requires calm actions on behalf of both divers. The technique requires the diver without air to share a companion's supply. This may be achieved in one of two ways.

If the assisting diver has an "Octopus" rig — that is a regulator which carries two second stages and, therefore, a spare mouthpiece — the second mouthpiece may be used by the diver without air, in order to reach the surface.

This technique cannot be solely relied on as not all divers use such a rig, although many instructors and more advanced divers will have this system. However, it is still possible to share air by "buddy breathing": two divers using one air supply and one mouthpiece. This technique ought to be part of any diver-training programme, as it can go wrong if both divers are not confident and competent in the sharing technique.

PRACTISING BUDDY BREATHING

Initially this will be carried out in a swimming pool or other shallow safe water.

Sit or kneel on the bottom and ensure that the donor's regulator is on the correct side, so it may be passed easily to the recipient without having to twist the tube. The diver out of air should signal to the rescuer that he needs air. The rescuer will then offer his mouthpiece, which should be gently purged to ensure a water-free delivery, at the same time taking a firm hold of his companion's harness to maintain contact.

After taking two or three breaths the mouthpiece should be passed back to the donor, who will take air and return the air supply once more to his companion. When not breathing from the mouthpiece both divers will gently exhale, simulating the essential ascent procedure of never holding breath when ascending.

This static sharing should be practised until both divers can share comfortably and without worry. They may then practise whilst swimming around the pool or in shallow water. Eventually they will advance to actual ascent practice using a shot line and, as always, supervised by a qualified instructor.

Fig 63

Buddy breathing should be practised on the pool bottom until both divers can share comfortably.

It is good practice for two divers sharing one air supply to both maintain contact with the mouthpiece by one placing a hand over the back of the diver's hand holding the mouthpiece or by gently holding the wrist. This will help guide the mouthpiece towards the diver's open mouth during the exchange.

Understanding Diving Physics

The very nature of the sport of diving removes man from his natural environment and places him in one which is alien. Water has effects upon the human body which need to be understood and compensated for. Some effects of pressure have already been discussed: mask squeeze, ear and sinus squeeze and suit compression will be understood from their obvious results.

The need to breathe normally when ascending, after having taken compressed air from an aqualung, has also been highlighted, as has the ability of the diver to change his buoyancy by simply breathing in or out. There are available a number of books, notably the British Sub-Aqua Club's Diving Manual "Sport Diving", which explain in much more detail Diving Physics and Physiology. However, here follows a brief explanation of a number of important facts.

VISION UNDERWATER
One result of fitting a pocket of air (mask) between the water and the diver's eye is to bend the light rays as they pass from the water to the air. This has the effect of making objects appear larger and closer than they are, an effect for which the diver soon learns to compensate.

SOUND
Water will act as an effective barrier to sound from above. However, underwater sounds travel at a much higher speed than they would in air — approximately five times faster. The diver's normal hearing will be confused by the speed in which sounds reach him, making it difficult, if not impossible, to determine their direction and source.

LIGHT ABSORBTION
Don't expect colour underwater to be as clear and well defined as in air. The deeper below the surface the less light penetrates thereby reducing the colour spectrum. As shallow as five metres

below the surface all reds will have gone; by 30 metres everything will appear grey. Providing an artificial light source will immediately bring out all the natural colour at any depth.

HEAT CONDUCTION
Water is a far more efficient conductor of heat than air is. In all but the warmest tropical waters a diver's body temperature will drop very rapidly with uncomfortable and eventually dangerous results.

Medical

OXYGEN SHORTAGE
The need for oxygen is a basic human requirement. The lack or shortage of the gas will lead to discomfort, distress and eventually demise. The human brain will not normally allow the neglect of continuous ventilation of the lungs and regularly passes messages which trigger the breathing process. Only accidental or deliberate interference with this process will stop normal breathing.

The snorkeller who holds his breath for long spells will soon be reminded of his need to breathe, unless he has deliberately tampered with the normal breathing mechanics by taking a series of deep breaths before starting the dive. These deep breaths, known technically as hyperventilation, have the effect of increasing the oxygen but reducing the other important gas in air, carbon dioxide, and there's the rub.

It's not shortage of oxygen that triggers the mechanism that makes us breathe, it's a build up of carbon dioxide. As a result of hyperventilation the brain misses the cue to pass the message — leaving the diver so low on oxygen that he can pass out. Below the surface that can be fatal. DON'T HYPERVENTILATE!

OXYGEN POISONING
Just as too little oxygen will be fatal for the diver, so will too much. Pure oxygen at depths below 8 metres becomes toxic. For more complex reasons even the oxygen in normal air will become toxic at depths of 80 metres or more. Neither of these facts will be a problem to a sports diver who will not be using pure oxygen underwater or be diving to depths of 80 metres.

NITROGEN NARCOSIS

The largest constituent gas in air is nitrogen. This gas has little use to a diver save for diluting oxygen. Nitrogen has a detrimental effect on the diver. It induces an intoxication that is akin to drunkenness, but occurs more rapidly and, when it passes, usually leaves no hangover.

Its effects vary with depth from mild euphoria and over-confidence to hallucinations, from confusion to stupor. Like a driver who has had alcohol, the diver with narcosis can be a danger to himself and others. Fortunately, nitrogen narcosis will not normally produce serious symptoms at sport diving depths above 30 metres.

Nitrogen has other effects on the diver which will be discussed later in the section "THE BENDS".

CARBON MONOXIDE

This deadly poison, colourless and odourless, should never be allowed to enter the diver's air supply. Produced by petrol and diesel engines as "exhaust", the gas can enter the supply from the air compressor used to fill the cylinder. An intelligent operator will be well aware of the dangers and will take all precautions to avoid this happening. Be cautious, use reputable air stations and watch out for engine fumes in the vicinity of the compressor intake.

The Bends

Almost everyone has heard of the "Bends" or, more correctly, decompression sickness. Whilst this is not the book to discuss the topic in great detail, it is important that the nature of the ailment is understood by any potential diver.

Decompression sickness is the result of nitrogen, that has been absorbed into the diver's blood and tissue under pressure, being allowed to decompress in an uncontrolled way. To understand this, consider the gas contained within lemonade and such drinks. It is invisible whilst kept under pressure, i.e. with the lid screwed down; but release the pressure too quickly and watch it fizz.

A diver who has been underwater has been under pressure. He must therefore return to the surface — decompress — in a controlled way, otherwise the nitrogen will start to form bubbles, that in turn will lead to decompression sickness.

The rate of absorbtion of gas into the diver's tissue is related to time spent below the surface and to the depth. The longer and deeper the dive, the greater the absorbtion of nitrogen, and the longer the time the diver must spend returning to the surface.

The important fact that must be remembered by every diver is that the time spent underwater is cumulative. Therefore, a diver undertaking a series of short dives is just as much at risk as a diver taking one longer dive.

Fortunately, timetables exist to enable a diver to calculate how long he may stay at any given depth without need for decompression stops. These are NO STOP TABLES. Likewise for the more advanced diver there are tables by which decompression stops can be calculated for longer or deeper dives.

These decompression tables are published by the British Sub-Aqua Club in co-operation with the Royal Navy Physiological Laboratory. They may be improved or revised from time to time.

For the purpose of this book it is recommended that all dives should be within the "No Stop Table". Remember that if more than one dive is made during the period of 12 hours, the times of all the dives added together must not be greater than the "No Stop Time". For the purpose of calculation, the deepest depth attained on any of the dives must be used.

Fig 64

RNPL/BSAC Air Diving Decompression Table

Descent Rate: 30 metres/minute maximum
Ascent Rate: 15 metres/minute

Maximum Depth (metres)	No Stop Time (minutes)	Bottom Time in Minutes					
10	232	431	—	—	—	—	—
12	137	140	159	179	201	229	270
14	96	98	106	116	125	134	144
16	72	73	81	88	94	99	105
18	57	59	66	71	76	80	84
20	46	49	55	60	63	67	70
Stops at 5 metres (minutes)		**5**	**10**	**15**	**20**	**25**	**30**
22	38	42	47	51	55	58	
24	32	37	41	45	48	51	
26	27	32	37	40	43	45	
28	23	29	33	36	39	41	
30	20	25	30	33	35	37	
32	18	23	27	30	32	34	
34	16	21	25	28	30	31	
36	14	20	23	26	27	29	
38	12	18	21	24	26	27	
40	11	17	20	22	24	25	
42	10	16	19	21	22	24	
44	9	15	18	20	21		
46	8	14	17	18	20		
48	8	13	16	17			
50	7	12	15	17			
Stops at 10 metres / 5 metres (minutes)		**5 / 5**	**5 / 10**	**5 / 15**	**5 / 20**	**5 / 25**	

Not more than 8 hours spent under pressure (submerged) during 24 hours

FOR TWO DIVES ONLY

When Second Dive is less than 9 metres no stop is required

A = Bottom Time in minutes of 1st Dive
B = Bottom Time in minutes of 2nd Dive

Both Dives less than 40 metres

Surface Interval	Bottom Time
Up to 2 hours	A + B
2 to 4 hours	$\frac{A}{2}$ + B
4 to 6 hours	$\frac{A}{4}$ + B
More than 6 hours	B

Either Dive more than 40 metres

Surface Interval	Bottom Time
Up to 2 hours	A + B
2 to 4 hours	$\frac{A}{2}$ + B
4 to 8 hours	$\frac{A}{4}$ + B
8 to 16 hours	$\frac{A}{8}$ + B
More than 16 hours	B

ALWAYS DECOMPRESS FOR THE GREATEST DEPTH REACHED DURING EITHER DIVE

DIVE DETAILS — Duration — Duration — Depth — Depth — Time — Time

PART 5

THE GREAT ADVENTURE

Diving from the Shore

Now all the basic training is behind you the adventuring begins
in earnest. The thrill of anticipation, that simply packing your diving
gear can engender, will be ten-fold when you arrive at your chosen
dive site — be it river, reservoir, lake or sea.

Looking down into the clear or, possibly, not so clear water will
arouse excitement and, maybe even a little trepidation. That's no
bad thing: care and a cautious approach are essential ingredients
of safe diving practice.

Preparing for the Dive

Preparation and attention to detail are the key to a comfortable and
safe dive. First the logistics. An organised approach to having your
diving equipment in the right place at the right time with the least
effort, will reduce hassle and help avoid the possibility of starting
your dive in an exhausted condition.

Sort out the details of the dive plan with your companion, ensure
the point of entry is accessible and, even more important, that there
are safe exit points. Do you know all that needs to be known about

tides, currents, depth, weather? Has shore cover been organised? Is visibility underwater adequate or will buddy lines be required?

Once the shore station is set up and dive pairs organised, it's time to "kit up". You ought, by now, to be developing a system for kitting up: each piece of gear checked and fitted in a logical and progressive order. The buddy system will also immediately come into play. Each assisting the other to dress for the dive, and — as part of the pre-dive brief — checking each other's equipment and air contents, and locating quick-release and buoyancy-inflation systems.

Brief over, signals exchanged with buddy and shore: into the water — probably walking in, fitting fins as late as possible — and down you go.

CONTACT: visual or physical contact should be maintained throughout the dive. Signals, even if only O.K. signals, should be exchanged on a regular basis.

PROGRESS: make the most of your visit to the underwater world. Slow, deliberate and observant progress will be much more rewarding than dashing hither and thither in a disorganised rush and probably missing more than you see.

Should visibility be poor reduce your dive area accordingly. Don't push on in the hope that it will get better — it won't. You will be amazed how much can be found in just a couple of square metres. Peep under rocks, look under kelp fronds and learn about your new environment. If you do see something of interest don't keep it to yourself, share it with your buddy. It's all part of the "underwater experience".

Leaving things where they are, for others to see and enjoy, is a good environmentalist diving code. Things which look beautiful below will often be a disappointment if dragged up to the shore.

Back to shore

The pre-arranged dive plan will have been made so that you return as near as possible to your starting or exit point for the completion of your dive. It's nice to pop-up near your exit rather than be faced with a long surface swim home.

Better also to finish a little earlier than planned than to overstay your time, even if you are enjoying yourself so much you don't want the dive to be over. Remember others are expecting you to return on time, and there could be other complications, such as decompression. If either buddy becomes cold, a natural awareness turns to anxiety or conditions deteriorate, the dive should be terminated. This will ensure that it has been an enjoyable experience, leaving you wanting more, not vowing "never again".

Once out of the water stow equipment and de-brief, have hot drinks, find warm clothes and start thinking about the next dive.

Diving from Boats

In essence, diving from boats is the same as shore diving. However, planning and preparation are far more significant. The diver who arrives at the dive-site, perhaps a long way from shore, and finds that an essential piece of equipment is in the boot of the car, will be most unpopular. Should you be diving from small boats handled by divers, the expedition will need to have been planned to a very high degree, considering all aspects of weather, sea conditions, tidal state, depth of water and timing.

For the passenger diving from a boat, the essential difference will be that entry will be directly into deeper water. There may be a little more tidal movement and the diver should know how to leave and re-enter the boat without difficulty.

ENTERING DEEPER WATER

This type of entry will depend on the size of boat. In larger boats a dive ladder will be provided. Entry from smaller boats will require the diver to jump or roll into the water. For example, the most popular entry from an inflatable boat is the backward roll where the diver falls backwards into the water, remembering to hold mask and mouthpiece in place.

Once in the water maintain contact with the boat by holding on to ropes or grab lines which should be provided. Should any current be running, even a very slight run, streaming lines should be available to ensure that divers don't drift away from the boat.

DESCENTS

In deeper water it is far safer to descend down a fixed line — either a weighted shot line or the anchor line of the boat.

Fig 65

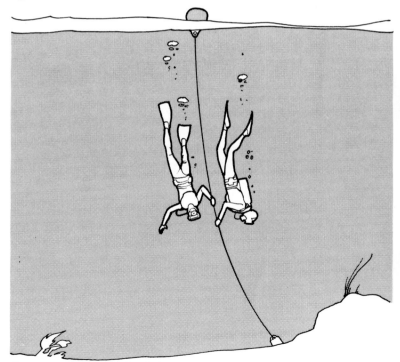

Descent using a weighted shot line.

Fig 66

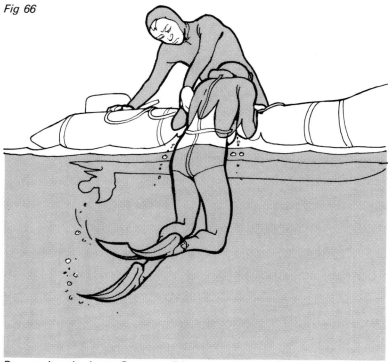

Re-entering the boat. Pass up all heavy equipment first.

RE-ENTERING THE BOAT

Re-entry to a small boat is best accomplished by first passing heavy equipment up to the boat. Keeping hold of the grab lines, pass up weight belt, S.M.B., aqualung, cameras etc. Keep mask and snorkel in place, and fin hard to assist you up and over the side.

If entering up a ladder, fins may have to be removed in order to negotiate the steps, making sure a firm hold is maintained of rail or safety line. Good underwater navigation is a great asset to the boat diver, saving long surface swims in what may be choppy waters.

The good boat diver will take to the boat all that will be required, but will not clutter the boat with unwanted equipment and will keep equipment tidy and out of the way both before *and* after the dive. Dive over and time for a hot drink — hope you remembered the flask! You will also have taken a windproof with you to keep you warm on the ride back.

Advancing Further

Advanced diving is beyond the intended scope of this book. However, it needs mentioning that, like the basic principles we have covered, advanced diving should be progressive. Move slowly on to more advanced techniques only when competent and experienced at the standard already reached.

Only a fool would make his first dive, on completion of pool training, down to a 30 metre wreck in cold dark water. Such an experience could be a discouragement from diving for ever. Yet the same dive, after a slow steady build up during a period of months, could be enjoyed by many.

The maxim should be: "Know your limitations and dive within them." Progress to advanced diving by building up experience whilst, at the same time, increasing your diving knowledge and learning new techniques, such as "roped diving", "navigation", "rescue and life saving".

ROPED DIVING

The roped diver is one who has his buddy on the other end of a life line, either on shore or in a boat. This technique is often used for working dives or where visibility is very poor.

Both diver and tender need to be practised in the use of lines and in the passing and receiving of signals along the line. The diver in the water is as dependent on his buddy as if he were next to him below the surface.

ROPE SIGNALS

Signals passed along the line are a series of pulls which must be understood by both parties. The basic signals, as recommended by the B.S.A.C., are:

	Surface Tender	Diver
1 Pull	Are you OK?	Yes I am OK.
2 Pulls	Stay put.	I am stationary.
3 Pulls	Go down.	I am going down.
4 Pulls	Come up.	I am coming up.
More than 4	Emergency — Bringing you up.	Emergency — Bring me up.

This is just one example of an advanced diving technique to illustrate how the sport diver can become more professional and may, eventually, progress to a professional diving career.

Diving Clubs

Most towns will have at least one sub-aqua club. Usually the best way to find these clubs is to enquire at your local swimming pool, where the club will probably meet and train.

The club will usually belong to the national body which in England, Wales and Northern Ireland is the British Sub-Aqua Club. The B.S.A.C. also have branches in Scotland and very many other countries throughout the world.

There are also a number of independent clubs, most of which follow the strict training standards set by their national body. Many of these clubs have now become members of an association of sub-aqua clubs: The Sub-Aqua Association. The S.A.A. have adopted similar diving standards to and training programmes of the other national clubs.

Training with a sub-aqua club will normally take longer than with a school as most clubs meet only once each week. However, pool and classroom lessons can be covered during the winter and prepare the trainee for the new spring and summer season. Each club has instructors who usually give their time and expertise freely. Most clubs provide equipment at a nominal cost for the newcomer to train with.

Diving clubs provide a social side to the sport and will enable members to make diving partnerships which are usually very enduring. The club will also own equipment, such as boats and air compressors for communal use.

Diving Schools

More and more diving schools open each year. Should you decide to opt for the more compact and concentrated course offered by a school you will be wise to choose a school which is recognised by the national body. This will ensure that any certification you receive, once you have completed your course, will be widely accepted.

The instructors in such a school will be qualified to a recognised international standard and will provide a certification upon which you will be able to build if you eventually join a club, or even take a more advanced course with your original or other recognised school.

Overseas Diving Centres

Throughout the world diving centres offer a whole range of diving opportunities. The Mediterranean coasts of France and Spain, North Africa, Cyprus, the Canaries, Balerics, the Red Sea and the Caribbean all have excellent centres.

Each will offer facilities for experienced divers who can provide proof of ability by log book or similar documentary evidence. Equipment hire, cylinder filling, boat hire, organised dive trips and safaries can all be arranged.

What more enjoyable way to learn to dive than to visit an overseas dive centre with a school facility, or to take a basic course at home and a more advanced course abroad? As with any dive school, make sure that the one you choose is recognised. Look for your own national organisation's approval or that of the Confederation Mondiale Des Activites Subaquatiques (C.M.A.S. or World Underwater Federation). This ensures your certification will be recognised when you return home.

BUYERS' GUIDE

Contents

ADVERTISERS

■ UK DIVING HOLIDAYS AND COURSES ■

LEARN TO DIVE—

IT'S FUN & EASY AT

Q DIVE

You need only 24 hours to learn to Dive.

Our courses are planned to suit your needs, complete in three days or stretched up to 8 weeks. Our nationally qualified instructors will introduce you to the world of underwater fun and adventure.

COME TO THE DIVING LOCKER AT Q DIVE FOR ALL YOUR WATERSPORT NEEDS

WE HAVE THE BEST CHOICE WITH THE BEST PRICES

We specialise in all types of watersports

—Snorkelling Equipment
  for your holidays
—Diving Equipment
—Waterskis and Accessories
—Windsurfing Wet Suits

Our expert and friendly advice is free
Q Dive at the Diving Locker is at:

Neptune House
43-49 Mortlake Road
Kew, Richmond
01-940 9194/9250

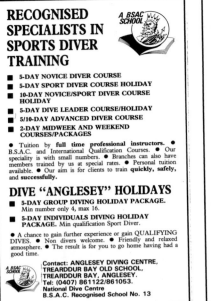

DIVING LEISURE

SHOP AND TRAINING FACILITY
THE TROPICANA POOL
ROCKLEY SANDS HOLIDAY ESTATE
HAMWORTHY
POOLE, DORSET, BH15 4LZ

POOLE (0202) 680898/673451 Ex 234
EVENINGS: WAREHAM (09295) 6106

LEARN TO SCUBA DIVE IN SIX DAYS

★ ALL EQUIPMENT PROVIDED
★ NO EXPERIENCE NECESSARY
★ FUN FOR ALL MEMBERS OF THE FAMILY OVER 14 YEARS OLD
★ GREAT TRAVEL OPPORTUNITIES
★ INTERNATIONAL OPEN WATER QUALIFICATION
★ PROFESSIONAL INSTRUCTORS FROM THE WORLD'S MOST SUCCESSFUL TRAINING AGENCY

FULL RANGE OF DIVING EQUIPMENT FOR SALE AT VERY COMPETITIVE PRICES

TRY A BOAT TRIP WITH A DIFFERENCE!

LUXURY 33' AQUASTAR, 'A' FLAG, FOR QUALIFIED DIVERS AND THEIR FAMILIES

★ INDIVIDUAL DIVERS AND SPECTATORS WELCOME
★ PROFESSIONAL SKIPPER
★ LARGE CHOICE OF WRECK AND REEF LOCATIONS
★ PAPERCHASE ECHOSOUNDER, MAGNETOMETER, NAVIGATOR, RADAR, VHF RADIO
★ LARGE DIVING PLATFORM
★ TOILET AND MODERN GALLEY
★ AIR
★ EQUIPMENT FOR SALE AND HIRE

DIVING

12½ acres of clear water. Terraced levels from 10ft – 120ft. Training installations include: Hydroboxes, Aircraft Cockpit, B.O.P., Hydro Trial Facilities and many others. Diving Times: 7 Days. Weekends 8.00am – 2.00 pm. Wednesday 9am – 4.00pm. Night Dive: 1st & 3rd Wednesday every month. Coaches please book.

SERVICES

Air to 3,700 psi. Cylinder Testing to BS 5430. Regulator Servicing to manufacturers spec. On-Site Recompression Chamber. Inflatable Boat Hire. Diver Training School. B.S.A.C, P.A.D.I., P.A.S.S. Lecture and Training Facilities.

REMEMBER!

Our Staff are available to advise and cater for your requirements and budgets. Access, Barclaycard and Lombard Finance.

SHOP

THE TRULY PROFESSIONAL SHOP. THE ONLY SUPPLIER OF THE NEW ORCA EDGE DIVE COMPUTER

Stocking: Hydrotech® , Humber, Tabata, Viking, Spiro, U.S.D., Poseidon, Scubapro, Cressi-Sub, Beaver, Luxfer, I.W.K.A., Sea Quest. We have an extensive range of Stab Jackets, Regulators, Cylinders, Instruments, Wet & Dry Suits, Masks, Fins and Snorkels, Gloves, Hoods, Boots and all Ancillary Equipment.

NEW!

SUPERBLY COMFORTABLE LEAD SHOT WEIGHT BELTS

**STONEY COVE MARINE TRIALS LTD
STONEY STANTON, LEICESTERSHIRE LE9 6DW
TEL: 045 527 3089.**

■ DIVING HOLIDAYS AND COURSES ABROAD ■

LEISUREDIVE WATERSPORTS AT
los cocoteros

READY TO TAKE THE SCUBA PLUNGE?

Then why not do so in the clear warm seas of the Canary Islands under the expert guidance of our enthusiastic scuba diving instructors who are there to make sure you enjoy your scuba diving experience to the full and you too will be able to safely marvel at the sights, sounds and sensations of the underwater world. And, if you wish, this can lead to international certification.

Have a friend who is already a qualified scuba diver? Then they can dive to their heart's content and revel in the many pleasures of diving in Lanzarote's rich waters.

And for a change of pace you can windsurf (or learn to!) or relax by our pool, taste the delights of our kitchens and bar, join us for barbecues on deserted beaches, explore the many sights of the island or simply relax in the privacy of your own self-catering apartamentos.

Unlike most other holidays, our standard price does not fluctuate with the season and includes your return flight from Gatwick, transfers to and from Arrecife airport, accommodation, the use of all scuba equipment and as many as 5 dives.

Tempted? Then write to us at Leisuredive Watersports Activity Holidays, c/o Box DFA/I, Diving For All, Underwater World Publications, 40 Gray's Inn Road, London WCIX 8LR.

HOLIDAYS FOR THE ACTIVELY DARING

79

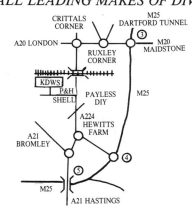

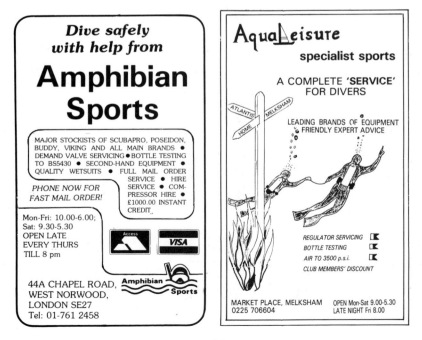

What's the Hottest thing Underwater this Year?

The Beaver Icelandic of course! With its superb thermal insulation, outstanding good looks, and exceptional popularity, it's the hottest item of underwater equipment available.

Your natural body heat is retained, and cold water is largely kept out, by the provision of efficient seals behind the zip, around the wrists, ankles and face, by new standards in tailoring, and by the use of the highest quality materials and stitching.

Add to that our expertise in manufacture, and the result is a semi-dry suit that 'Diver' has described as 'a Rolls-Royce amongst wet suits.'

For your nearest stockist and further information, write to:

BEAVER SPORTS (YORKS.) LTD.
Flint Street, Fartown, Huddersfield
West Yorkshire
or telephone
(0484) 512354

BEAVER

THE INNOVATORS

INDEX OF ADVERTISERS' PRODUCTS AND SERVICES

Nautilus/Oceanic   (Full range)
Scubapro   (Full range)
Shark Sports/Tekna   (Diving suits/Full range)
Viking/Cyalume   (Drysuits/Light sticks)

DIVING HOLIDAYS — ABROAD
Cydive   (Cyprus)
Leisure Dive   (Lanzarote)
Maltaqua   (Malta)
Sea Gozo   (Gozo)
Seychelles Underwater Centre   (Seychelles)
Twickers World   (Various countries)

DIVING HOLIDAYS — UK
Anglesey Diving Centre   (Anglesey, Wales)
Devon Offshore   (Devon)
Northburn Caravan Park   (Eyemouth, Scotland)
The Poole Dive Centre   (Dorset)
The Sands Motel   (Orkney, Scotland)
Tralee Bay Holidays   (Oban, Scotland)

CHARTER BOATS
Devon Offshore   (Devon)
Diving Leisure   (Dorset)
Northburn Caravan Park   (Eyemouth, Scotland)
Southern Marine Services   (West Sussex)
The Poole Dive Centre   (Dorset)
The Sands Motel   (Orkney, Scotland)

MANUFACTURERS & DISTRIBUTORS
Apeks Marine Equipment Ltd
Beaver Sports (Yorks) Ltd
Collins & Chambers Ltd
Midland Diving Equipment Ltd
Scubapro (UK) Ltd
Shark Sports Ltd
Sub Sea Services Ltd

SPECIALISED COURSES
Devon Offshore   (Chartwork & navigation)
Northburn Caravan Park   (Underwater photography)
Radio School   (Marine radio)

GLOSSARY

A.B.L.J.: Adjustable Buoyancy Life Jacket.

ABSOLUTE PRESSURE: The sum of atmospheric and water pressure.

AQUALUNG: Equipment containing compressed air used for underwater swimming.

ATMOSPHERE: Air surrounding earth. Also term in physics relating to pressure produced by that air. 1 Atmosphere = 14.7 lb per sq inch (used pre-decimalisation).

BAR: Measurement of pressure surrounding earth, used post-decimalisation (Barometric Pressure) 1 Bar = 1,000 millibars.

BASIC EQUIPMENT: Equipment used for snorkel diving and part of that required for aqualung diving: mask, fins and snorkel tube.

BENDS: Suffered by divers who dive too deep and/or too long. Caused by too rapid decompression of nitrogen in tissue and blood. Also correctly known as decompression sickness.

BOTTLE: See CYLINDER.

BUDDY: Diving companion.

BUDDY BREATHING: Emergency drill: two divers using one breathing set.

BUDDY LINE: Short contact line used by buddies in low visibility.

BUDDY SYSTEM: Safety system for divers who will always dive with a buddy.

BUOYANCY CONTROL: Ability of diver to control position underwater by adjusting buoyancy.

CLEARING EARS: Technique of equalising pressure in middle ear.

CLEARING SNORKEL: The removal of water from flooded snorkel tube.

COMPRESSOR: For compressing air to fill aqualung.

CONTENTS GAUGE: Gauge attached to aqualung which indicates pressure of air contained.

CRAB HOOK: Bar with handle at one end and bend at other, used for crab fishing.

CYCLING: Poor finning technique.

CYLINDER: Container for compressed air.

DEMAND VALVE: Valve which provides air underwater at pressure required and on "Demand". Part of aqualung.

DEPTH GAUGE: Gauge indicating depth of diver below surface.

DISPLACEMENT CLEARING: System of clearing water from mask or snorkel tube by displacing it with air.

DUCK DIVE: Head-first dive from surface.

DRY SUIT: Diving dress to keep diver dry.

E.A.R.: Expired Air Resuscitation: life-saving technique.

E.C.M.: External Cardiac Massage: life-saving technique.

EUSTACHIAN TUBE: Connecting tube between back of throat and middle ear; enables "ear clearing" to take place.

EXHAUST VALVE: Part of demand valve which permits diver's used air to escape.

FIN: Foot paddle used by divers and snorkellers.

FIRST STAGE: Part of demand valve; reduces high pressure air to medium pressure.

FIX PALM: 'Y' shaped strap for retaining fin on diver's foot.

FROGMAN: Wartime name for underwater swimmer.

HARNESS: Part of aqualung to attach set to diver.

HIGH PRESSURE HOSE: Carries air direct from diver's cylinder bottle to demand valve and contents gauge.

HYPERVENTILATION: Deep and rapid breathing that flushes carbon dioxide from lungs, making it possible to over-ride desire to breathe. Dangerous practice for snorkellers and divers.

JACKNIFE DIVE: Surface dive where diver or snorkeller jacknifes from waist (see Duck Dive).

KELP: Long wide-frond seaweed, common around UK coast.

LIFEJACKET: Inflatable life vest used by divers and snorkellers.

LIFELINE: Thin strong line attached to diver when diving solo, controlled by surface tender.

MEDIUM PRESSURE HOSE: Carries medium pressure from first to second stage of demand valve.

METRE: Unit of measurement: 1,000th part of a kilometre.

MOUTH BREATHING: Practised by divers and snorkellers when nose is covered by mask.

NITROGEN NARCOSIS: Narcotic effect caused by breathing compressed air at depth.

NO STOP TABLE: Table of times and depths from which it is considered safe to ascend without decompression stops.

OCTOPUS RIG: Demand valve that has more than one second stage for use in emergency.

OXYGEN SET: Breathing apparatus that feeds diver pure oxygen. Used by service divers during wartime. Not safe for sport diving.

PILLAR VALVE: Valve attached to neck of aqualung cylinder which allows air to be turned on and off.

PURGE BUTTON: Button that, when pressed, allows air to free-flow through demand valve, purging out water.

QUICK-RELEASE: Type of fastening that must be fitted to all weight belts and aqualung harnesses.

REGULATOR: Another name for Demand Valve.

RESERVE VALVE: Valve fitted to aqualung that holds back part of air supply until required as reserve.

S.C.U.B.A.: Self-Contained Underwater Breathing Apparatus — American term for aqualung.

S.L.J.: Surface Life Jacket: not suitable for divers.

S.M.B.: Surface Marker Buoy: carried by divers to mark their position.

SECOND STAGE: Part of demand valve that houses mouthpiece and purge button; delivers air to diver at pressure required.

SHOT LINE: Rope with float and heavy weight used by divers for ascending and decending.

SNORKEL TUBE: Open-ended tube used by divers and snorkellers for easy breathing at surface.

SQUEEZE: Effect of underwater pressure on air spaces in divers body and equipment.

STREAMING LINE: Light line trailed out behind diving boat and used as a grab-line for divers when current is running.

TANK: Another name for diving cylinder or bottle.

WEIGHT BELT: Waist belt to which weights are fitted.

WET SUIT: Tight-fitting diving suit that allows water to enter.